SPANISH ON THE JOB

Southwestern Press
800 Grand Avenue, Suite AG-8166
Carlsbad, California 92008

Published by
Southwestern Press
800 Grand Avenue, Suite AG-8166
Carlsbad, California 92008
(619) 434-8858

ISBN 0-923176-09-8
Library of Congress Catalog Number
90-158846

INTRODUCTION

How do you communicate with a Spanish-speaking worker if you don't speak Spanish?

SPANISH ON THE JOB – a Quick Easy Word Guide offers employers the immediate ability to communicate with the Spanish-speaking employees.

Written to "get the work done," this thorough yet concise guide will maximize understanding, especially in the construction, landscaping, and housekeeping trades.

Each entry appears in English and Spanish and is phonetically spelled out to assure correct pronunciation. **No previous knowledge of Spanish is necessary.**

TABLE OF CONTENTS

Part I

COMMON WORDS AND PHRASES

COMMON WORDS AND PHRASES

MONEY

EL DINERO
el de-NEH-row

CASH	en efectivo **en eh-fech-TEE-voh**
CHECK	el cheque **el CHEH-kay**
DO YOU NEED AN ADVANCE?	¿Necesitas un avance? **neh-seh-SEE-tahs oon ah-VAHN-say**
DO YOU NEED MONEY?	¿Necesitas dinero? **neh-seh-SEE-tahs de-NEH-row**
HOW MUCH?	¿Cuánto? **KWAN-toe**
MONEY ORDER	el giro postal **el HEE-roh poh-STAHL**
I PAY ___ AN HOUR.	Pago ___ la hora. **PAH-go ___ la OH-rah**
A DAY	el día **el DEE-ah**
A WEEK	la semana **la say-MAH-nah**
A MONTH	el mes **el mess**
PLUS ROOM AND BOARD	más el cuarto y comida **mahs el KWAR-toh ee co-ME-dah**

SPANISH ON THE JOB

$5.00	cinco dólares **SEEN-koh DOE-la-rehs**
$5.25	cinco veinticinco **SEEN-koh vain-tee-SEEN-koh**
$5.50	cinco cincuenta **SEEN-koh seen-KWHEN-tah**
$5.75	cinco setenta y cinco **SEEN-koh seh-TEHN-tah ee SEEN-koh**
$6.00	seis dólares **sase DOE-la-rehs**
$30.00	treinta dólares **treh-IN-tah DOE-la-rehs**
$40.00	cuarenta dólares **kwah-REHN-tah DOE-la-rehs**
$45.00	cuarenta y cinco dólares **kwah-REHN-tah SEEN-koh DOE-la-rehs**
$100.00	cien dólares **see-YEHN DOE-la-rehs**
$102.00	ciento dos dólares **see-YEHN-toe dohs DOE-la-rehs**

COMMON WORDS AND PHRASES

$140.00	ciento cuarenta **see-YEHN-toe** **kwah-REHN-tah**
$200.00	doscientos **dohs-see-YEHN-tohs**
$300.00	trescientos **trehs-see-YEHN-tohs**
$400.00	cuatrocientos **kwah-troh-see-YEHN-tohs**
$500.00	quinientos **keen-NYEN-tohs**
$600.00	seiscientos **sase-see-YEHN-tohs**
$700.00	setecientos **seh-teh-see-YEHN-tohs**
$800.00	ochocientos **oh-choh-see-YEHN-tohs**
$900.00	novecientos **noh-veh-see-YEHN-tohs**
$1000.00	mil **meel**

SPANISH ON THE JOB

I PAY EVERY ____ .   Se paga ____ .
                          say PAH-gah ____ .

I WILL PAY YOU ON ____ .   Te pagaré el ____ .
                               teh pah-gah-RAY el ____ .

SUNDAY	el domingo **el doh-MEEN-goh**
MONDAY	el lunes **el LOO-nehs**
TUESDAY	el martes **el MAHR-tehs**
WEDNESDAY	el miércoles **el me-YEHR-koh-lehs**
THURSDAY	el jueves **el HWEH-vehs**
FRIDAY	el viernes **el ve-YEHR-nehs**
SATURDAY	el sábado **el SAH-bah-doh**

COMMON WORDS AND PHRASES

THE COLORS

LOS COLORES
lohs co-LOR-ehs

BLACK

negro
NAY-gro

BLUE

azul
ah-SOOL

BROWN

café
kah-FEH

DARK

oscuro
os-COO-roh

GRAY

gris
grease

GREEN

verde
VER-deh

LIGHT	claro **CLAH-roh**
ORANGE	naranja **nah-RAHN-ha**
PURPLE	morado **mo-RAH-doh**
RED	rojo **ROW-hoe**
WHITE	blanco **BLAN-coh**
YELLOW	amarillo **ah-mah-REE-yoh**

COMMON WORDS AND PHRASES

TIME

LA HORA
la OH-ra

BE HERE AT _____ .	Este aquí a la(s) _____ . **ES-teh ah-KEY** **ah la(s) _____ .**

QUIT AT _____ .	Para a la(s) _____ . **PAH-rah ah la(s) _____ .**

START WORK AT _____ .	Empieza a trabajar a la(s) _____ . **em-pe-EH-sah** **ah tra-ba-HAR** **ah la(s) _____ .**

WHAT TIME IS IT?	¿Qué hora es? **keh OH-rah es**

YOU MAY LEAVE AT _____ .	Te puedes ir a la(s) _____ . **tey PWEH-des ear** **ah la(s) _____ .**

1:00	es la una **es la OO-nah**

1:15	es la una y cuarto **es la OO-nah** **ee KWAR-toh**

1:30	es la una y media **es la OO-nah** **ee MEH-dyah**

SPANISH ON THE JOB

1:45	es la una y cuarenta y cinco **es la OO-nah ee kwa-REN-tah ee SEEN-koh**
2:00	son las dos **sohn lahs dohs**
3:00	son las tres **sohn lahs trehs**
4:00	son las cuatro **sohn lahs KWAH-troh**
5:00	son las cinco **sohn lahs SEEN-koh**
6:00	son las seis **sohn lahs sase**
7:00	son las siete **sohn lahs see-YEH-teh**
8:00	son las ocho **sohn lahs OH-cho**
9:00	son las nueve **sohn lahs noo-EH-veh**
10:00	son las diez **sohn lahs dee-YES**
11:00	son las once **sohn lahs OHN-seh**

COMMON WORDS AND PHRASES

12:00	son las doce **sohn lahs DOH-seh**
YOU WILL HAVE SUNDAY OFF.	Descansarás los domingos. **dehs-cahn-sah-RAHS lohs doh-MEEN-gohs.**
MONDAY	los lunes **lohs LOO-nehs**
TUESDAY	los martes **lohs MAHR-tes**
WEDNESDAY	los miércoles **lohs me-YEHR-koh-lehs**
THURSDAY	los jueves **lohs HWEH-vehs**
FRIDAY	los viernes **lohs ve-YEHR-nehs**
SATURDAY	los sábados **lohs SAH-bah-dohs**
YOU WILL WORK _____ HOURS. DAYS. MONTHS.	Vas a trabajar _____ horas. días. meses. **vahs ah trah-ba-HAR _____ OH-rahs. DEE-ahs. MEH-sehs.**

SPANISH ON THE JOB

TIME

AFTERNOON	tarde **TAHR-deh**
DAY	día **DEE-ah**
HOUR	hora **OH-rah**
MIDNIGHT	medianoche **meh-dee-ah-NO-chay**
MINUTE	minuto **me-NOO-toh**
MONTH	mes **mess**
MORNING	mañana **mah-NYAH-nah**
NEXT WEEK	semana que viene **seh-MAH-nah kay vee-EN-neh**
NOON	mediodía **meh-de-oh-DEE-ah**
NIGHT	noche **NO-chay**

COMMON WORDS AND PHRASES

TODAY

hoy
oy
este día
ES-teh DE-ah

TOMORROW

mañana
mah-NYAH-nah

WEEK

semana
seh-MAH-nah

YEAR

año
AHN-yoh

YESTERDAY

ayer
ah-YER

THE MONTHS

LOS MESES
lohs MEH-sehs

JANUARY	enero **eh-NEH-roh**
FEBRUARY	febrero **feh-BREH-roh**
MARCH	marzo **MAHR-soh**
APRIL	abril **ah-BREEL**
MAY	mayo **MAH-yoh**
JUNE	junio **hoo-NEE-oh**
JULY	julio **hoo-LEE-oh**
AUGUST	agosto **ah-GOHS-toh**
SEPTEMBER	septiembre **sep-te-YEHM-breh**
OCTOBER	octubre **ohk-TOO-breh**

COMMON WORDS AND PHRASES

NOVEMBER	noviembre **noh-ve-YEHM-breh**
DECEMBER	diciembre **de-see-YEHM-breh**

THE DAYS

LOS DÍAS
lohs DEE-ahs

MONDAY	lunes **LOO-nehs**
TUESDAY	martes **MAHR-tehs**
WEDNESDAY	miércoles **me-YEHR-koh-lehs**
THURSDAY	jueves **HWEH-vehs**
FRIDAY	viernes **ve-YEHR-nehs**
SATURDAY	sábado **SAH-bah-doh**
SUNDAY	domingo **doh-MEEN-goh**

SPANISH ON THE JOB

THE NUMBERS

0	cero **SEH-roh**
1	uno **OO-noh**
2	dos **dohs**
3	tres **trehs**
4	cuatro **KWAH-troh**
5	cinco **SEEN-koh**
6	seis **sase**
7	siete **see-YEH-teh**
8	ocho **OH-choh**

COMMON WORDS AND PHRASES

9	nueve **noo-EH-veh**
10	diez **dee-YES**
11	once **OHN-seh**
12	doce **DOH-seh**
13	trece **TREH-seh**
14	catorce **kah-TOHR-seh**
15	quince **KEEN-seh**
16	diez y seis **dee-YES ee sase**
17	diez y siete **dee-YES ee see-YEH-teh**
18	diez y ocho **dee-YES ee OH-choh**
19	diez y nueve **dee-YES ee noo-EH-veh**

SPANISH ON THE JOB

20	veinte **VAIN-teh**
21	veinte y uno **VAIN-teh ee OO-noh**
30	treinta **treh-IN-tah**
40	cuarenta **kwah-REHN-tah**
50	cincuenta **seen-KWEHN-tah**
60	sesenta **seh-SEHN-tah**
70	setenta **seh-TEHN-tah**
80	ochenta **oh-CHEHN-tah**
90	noventa **noh-VEHN-tah**
100	cien **see-YEHN**
1000	mil **meel**

COMMON WORDS AND PHRASES

FIRST	primero **pre-MEH-roh**
SECOND	segundo **seh-GOON-doh**
THIRD	tercero **ter-SEH-roh**
FOURTH	cuarto **QUAR-toh**
FIFTH	quinto **KEEN-toh**
SIXTH	sexto **SEK-toh**
SEVENTH	séptimo **SEP-tee-moh**
EIGHTH	octavo **ok-TAH-voh**
NINTH	noveno **no-VEH-noh**
TENTH	décimo **DEH-see-moh**

WORDS AND PHRASES

ACROSS	a través **ah trah-VESS**
AFTER, LATER **AFTERWARDS**	después **des-PWES**
AGAIN	otra vez **OH-tra vess** de nuevo **deh NWAY-voh**
ALL	todo **TOE-doe**
BACK (FRONT)	atrás **ah-TROSS**
BAD	malo **MAH-low**
BEFORE	antes **AHN-tess**

COMMON WORDS AND PHRASES

BEGIN, TO	empieza (you) **em-pe-EH-sah** empezar (to) **em-peh-SAR**
BELOW	abajo **ah-BAH-ho** debajo **deh-BAH-ho**
BETTER	mejor **meh-HORE**
BIG	grande **GRAHN-day**
BORDER PATROL	la migra **la MEE-grah**
BOTH	los dos **lohs dohs**
BOTTOM	fondo **FOHN-doh**
BRING, TO	trae (you) **TRAH-eh** traer (to) **trah-ERR**

SPANISH ON THE JOB

BUY, TO	compra (you) **KOHM-pra** comprar (to) **kohm-PRAHR**
CAR	carro **CAR-row**
CARE, CAREFUL	cuidado **kwe-DAH-doe**
CAREFULLY	cuidadosamente **kwe-dah-doe-sah-MEN-teh**
CLEAN	limpio **leem-PEE-oh**
CLEAN THIS UP	limpia esto **leem-PEE-ah ES-toh**
CLEAN UP, TO	limpia (you) **leem-PEE-ah** limpiar (to) **leem-pee-ARE**
CLOSED	cerrado **seh-RAH-doe**
COFFEE	el café **el kah-FEH**
COLD	frío **FREE-oh**

COMMON WORDS AND PHRASES

COME, TO	ven (you) **vhen** venir (to) **vhen-EAR**
COME HERE!	¡Ven aquí! **VHEN ah-KEY** ¡Ven acá! **VHEN ah-CAH**
DANGEROUS	peligroso **peh-lee-GROSS-oh**
DEEP	profundo **pro-FOON-doe**
DINNER	la cena **la SEN-ah**
DO IT LIKE THIS.	Hágalo así. **AH-gah-lo ah-SEE**
DOLLAR	el dólar **el DOE-lahr**
DOWN	abajo **ah-BAH-hoh**

DRINK, TO	beber (to) **beh-BEAR** toma (you) **TOE-mah** tomar (to) **toe-MAR**
DRY	seco **SEH-koh**
DRY, TO	secar **seh-CAR**
EAT, TO	come (you) **KOH-may** comer (to) **koh-MEHR**
EMPTY	vacio **vah-SEE-oh**
END, THE	el fin **el FEEN**
END, TO	terminar **tear-me-NAR**
ENOUGH (PLENTY)	bastante **bahs-TAHN-tey**
ENTRANCE	entrada **ehn-TRA-dah**

COMMON WORDS AND PHRASES

EXIT	salida **sah-LEE-dah**
FAST	rápido **RAH-pee-doe**
FEW (A LITTLE)	poco **POH-koh**
FILL, TO	llena (you) **YEH-nah** llenar (to) **yeh-NAR**
FIND, TO	halla (you) **AYE-yah** hallar (to) **aye-YAR**
FOLLOW ME	Sígame **SEE-gah-meh**
FRONT	en frente **ehn FREN-tay**
FULL	lleno **YEN-oh**
GET, (FETCH)	trae (you) **TRAH-eh** busca (you) **BOOS-cah**

SPANISH ON THE JOB

GO	ve **VEH**
GOOD	bueno **BWAY-noh**
GOOD, THAT'S	Está bien **es-TAH** **be-EN**
GOOD BYE	adiós **ah-dee-YOHS**
HEAVY	pesado **peh-SAH-doe**
HELLO	hola **OH-lah**
HELP, TO	ayuda (you) **ah-YOU-dah** ayudar (to) **ah-yoo-DAR**
HERE	aquí **ah-KEY**
HIGH	alto **AHL-toe**
HOT	caliente **kah-lee-EN-tay**

COMMON WORDS AND PHRASES

HOW DO YOU SAY?	¿Cómo se dice? **KOH-moh seh DEE-say**
HOW MANY?	¿Cuántos? **KWAN-tohs**
HOW MUCH?	¿Cuánto? **KWAN-toh**
HOW OLD?	¿Cuántos años? **KWAN-tohs AH-nyos**
HUNGRY, ARE YOU?	¿Tienes hambre? **tee-EN-es AHM-bray**
HURRY UP!	¡apúrate! **ah-POO-rah-teh**
HURT, INJURY	daño **DAHN-yo** herida **err-EE-dah**
IMMIGRATION DEPARTMENT	la migra **la MEE-grah**
IN	en **ehn**
INSIDE	adentro **ah-DEN-tro**

SPANISH ON THE JOB

JACKET	la chaqueta **la chak-ET-ah**
JUICE	el jugo **el HOO-go**
LAST	último **OOL-tea-moe**
LATE	tarde **TAR-deh**
LEAVE, TO	vete (you) **VEH-teh** irse (to) **EAR-seh**
LEAVE (OBJECT BEHIND)	dejar (to) **deh-HAR**
LEFT (RIGHT)	izquierdo **ees-key-AIR-doe**
LEGAL, ARE YOU?	¿Tienes papeles? **tee-EN-es** **pah-PEL-es**
LITTLE	chico **CHEE-koh**
LONG	largo **LAR-go**

COMMON WORDS AND PHRASES

LOOK FOR, TO	busca (you) **BOOS-cah** buscar (to) **boos-CAR**
LOOK OUT!	¡Cuidado! **kwe-DAH-doe**
LUNCH	el almuerzo **el al-MWARE-soh** la merienda **la merry-END-ah**
MAKE, TO	haz (you) **ahs** hacer (to) **ah-SEHR**
MAN	hombre **OM-bray**
ME	me **meh**
MIDDLE	medio **meh-DEE-oh**
MINE	mío **MEE-oh**
MOIST	húmedo **HOO-meh-doe**

SPANISH ON THE JOB

MORE	más **mahs**
MOVE, TO	mueve (you) **MWAY-vay** mover (to) **mow-VAIR**
MUCH	mucho **MOO-choh**
NAME	el nombre **el NOM-bray**
NEAR TO	cerca de **SER-kah deh**
NEED	necesidad **ness-cess-e-DAHD**
NEVER	nunca **NOON-kah**
NEW	nuevo **NWAY-voh**
NEXT	próximo **PROX-e-moe**
NO	no **noh**

COMMON WORDS AND PHRASES

NOTHING	nada **NAH-dah**
NOW	ahora **ah-OH-rah**
OFF (TO TURN)	apaga (you) **ah-PAH-gah** apagar (to) **ah-pah-GAHR**
OKAY	bien **be-EN**
OLD	viejo **ve-EH-hoh**
ON	en **ehn**
ON (OFF)	prendido **pren-DEE-doh**
ONLY	único **OO-nee-co** sólo **SO-loh** no más **noh mahs**
OPEN	abierto **ah-bee-EHR-toh**

SPANISH ON THE JOB

OPEN, TO	abrir **ah-BREER**
OTHER	otro **OH-troh**
OUT	fuera **FWAY-rah**
OVER	por encima **poor en-SEE-mah** encima de **en-SEE-mah deh**
PAY	paga **PAH-gah**
PAY, TO	pago (I) **PAH-go** pagar (to) **pah-GAR**
PAY ATTENTION	ponga atención **PON-ga** **ah-ten-see-OHN**
PLEASE	por favor **poor fah-VOR**
PULL, TO	jala (you) **AH-lah** jalar (to) **ah-LAR**

COMMON WORDS AND PHRASES

PUSH, TO	empuja (you) **em-POO-ha**
	empujar (to) **em-poo-HAR**
PUT, TO	pon (you) **pohn**
	poner (to) **poh-NER**
QUICK	rápido **RAH-pee-doe**
	pronto **PROHN-toh**
QUIT, TO	dejar **deh-HAR**
	de hacer **deh ah-CEHR**
READ, CAN YOU?	¿Puedes leer? **PWAY-dehs leh-ERR**
REMAIN, TO	quédese (you) **KAY-deh-seh**
	quedarse (to) **kay-DAHR-seh**
REMEMBER, TO	recuerda (you) **reh-QWEAR-dah**
	recordar (to) **reh-core-DAR**

SPANISH ON THE JOB

RIGHT (LEFT)	derecha **deh-REH-chah**
RIGHT (WRONG)	correcto **co-REHC-toe** bien **be-EN**
SAME	igual **e-GWALL**
SHALLOW (DEPTH)	poco hondo **POH-koh OHN-doh**
SHARP (NOT DULL)	filoso **fee-LO-soh**
SHORT (HEIGHT)	bajo **BA-hoe**
SHORT (LENGTH)	corto **CORE-toe**
SHUT	cierra (you) **see-EH-rah** cerrar (to) **ser-RAHR**
SLOW	lento **LEN-toe**
SMALL	pequeño **peh-KEHN-yo**

COMMON WORDS AND PHRASES

SOCIAL SECURITY NUMBER	número de seguro social **NOO-meh-row deh seh-GOO-roh soh-see-ALL**
SORRY	perdón **per-DOHN** lo siento **lo see-EN-toe**
SPANISH	Español **ehs-pahn-YOHL**
SPEAK ENGLISH?, DO YOU	¿Hablas inglés? **AB-lahs in-GLAYS**
STACK, TO	apilar **ah-pee-LAR**
START, TO	empieza (you) **em-pe-EH-sah** empezar (to) **em-peh-SAR**
START HERE	empieza aquí **em-pe-EH-sah ah-KEY**
STOP	para **PAH-rah**
TAKE, TO	tomar **toe-MAR**

SPANISH ON THE JOB

THANK YOU	gracias **grah-SEE-ahs**
THAT	ese **ES-eh** esa **ES-ah**
THAT'S ALL	eso es todo **ES-so es TOE-doe**
THERE	allí **ah-YE**
THICK	espeso **ess-PES-so** grueso **groo-EH-so**
THIN	delgado **del-GA-doe** flaco **FLAH-co**
THIS	este **ES-teh** esta **ES-tah**
TO	para **PAH-rah**

COMMON WORDS AND PHRASES

TRY, TO	trata (you) **TRAH-tah** tratar (to) **trah-TAR**
UNDER	debajo **deh-BAH-hoe**
UNDERSTAND	comprende **kohm-PREN-deh**
UNTIE, TO	desata (you) **deh-SAH-tah** dasatar (to) **deh-sah-TAR**
UP, ABOVE, TOP	arriba **ah-REE-bah**
USE, TO	usa (you) **OOS-ah** usar (to) **oos-ARE**
VERY	muy **moo-EE**
WAIT HERE.	Espera aquí. **es-PEH-rah** **ah-KEY**
WANT, DO YOU?	¿Quieres? **key-err-ES**

SPANISH ON THE JOB

WARM	tibio **tee-BEE-yo**
WARM, TO	calentar **kah-lehn-TAR**
WATCH ME	Mírame **MEE-rah-meh**
WATCH OUT!	¡Cuidado! **kwe-DAH-doe**
WEAR, TO	llevar **yeh-VAR**
WELCOME, YOU ARE	de nada **deh NA-dah**
WELL DONE	muy bien **moo-EE be-EN**
WHAT?	¿Qué? **keh**
WHAT IS YOUR NAME?	¿Cómo te llamas? **KO-mo tay YA-mahs**
WHERE?	¿Dónde? **DOHN-day**
WHEN?	¿Cuándo? **KWAN-doe**

COMMON WORDS AND PHRASES

WHO?	¿Quién? **key-EHN**
WHY?	¿Por qué? **poor keh**
WIDE	ancho **AHN-cho**
WITH	con **kohn**
WITHOUT	sin **seen**
WOMAN	mujer **moo-HAIR**
WORD	palabra **pa-LA-bra**
WORK	trabajo **tra-BAH-hoe**
WRITE, TO	escribe (you) **es-CREE-beh** escribir (to) **es-cre-BEER**
WRITE?, CAN YOU	¿Puedes escribir? **poo-EH-dehs** **es-cre-BEER**

SPANISH ON THE JOB

WRONG	incorrecto **in-cor-REC-toh** malo **MAH-lo**
YES	sí **see**
YOU	tú **to** usted **oo-STED**

Part II

CONSTRUCTION

CONSTRUCTION	CONSTRUCCIÓN cohn-strooc-see-OHN
AIR	aire **EYE-rey**
ANGLE	ángulo **AHN-goo-lo**
AREA	área **AH-reh-ah**
ATTACH, TO	juntar **hoon-TAR** pegar **pay-GAR**
AXE	el hacha **el AH-cha**
BARRICADE	barricada **bar-ee-CAH-dah**
BASEMENT	el sótano **el SOH-tahn-oh**
BATHTUB	la bañera **la bahn-NYEH-rah**
BEND, TO	doblar **doe-BLAR**
BLADE (SAW)	la hoja del serrucho eléctrico **la OH-ha del serr-RU-cho** **el-LEC-tree-co**

SPANISH ON THE JOB

BLOCK	bloque **BLO-kay**
BOLT	perno **PEAR-no** tornillo grueso **tore-KNEE-yoh** **groo-EH-so**
BOX	la caja **la CAH-ha**
BRACE	grapón **grah-POHN** reforzador **ray-for-sah-DOOR**
BREAK, TO	romper **rohm-PARE** quebrar **kay-BRAR**
BRICK	el ladrillo **el la-DREE-yoh**
BROKEN	roto **ROH-toe** quebrado **kay-BRA-doh**
BROOM	la escoba **la es-COH-bah**

CONSTRUCTION

BRUSH	el cepillo **el seh-PEE-yoh**
BUCKET	la cubeta **la coo-BEH-tah** el balde **el BALL-deh**
BUILDING	el edificio **el eh-de-FEE-see-oh**
BURN, TO	quemar **kay-MAR**
CABINET	el gabinete **el gah-bee-NEH-teh**
CABLE	el cable **el CAH-blay**
CARPENTER	carpintero **car-peen-TEH-roh**
CARPET	la carpeta **la car-PET-ah**
CAULK	goma para sellar o resanar **GO-ma PAH-rah** **say-YAR o reh-sah-NAR**
CEILING	el techo **el TEH-cho**

CEMENT	el cemento **el seh-MEN-toh**
CENTER	el centro **el SEN-tro**
CHAIN	la cadena **la cah-DEH-nah**
CHAIN SAW	la sierra de cadena **la see-ERR-ah** **deh cah-DEH-nah**
CHALK	la tiza **la TEA-sah** el gis **el heese**
CHANNEL	la canal **la cah-NAL**
CHISEL	el cincel **el sceen-SELL** el formón **el for-MOHN**
CHOP, TO	tajar **tah-HAR** picar **pea-CAR**

CIRCLE	el círculo **el SEAR-coo-lo**
CLAMP	la prensa de sujetar **la PREN-sah deh sue-hay-TAR**
CLEAN, TO	limpiar **leem-pee-ARE**
CLIMB UP	subir **sue-BEER** escalar **es-cah-LAR**
COMPRESSOR	compresor de aire **comb-PRESS-ore deh EYE-rey**
CONNECT, TO	conectar **co-neck-TAR**
CORNER	la esquina **la es-KEY-nah**
CRACK	grieta **gree-EH-tah**
CUT, TO	cortar **cohr-TAR**
DANGER	peligro **peh-LEE-groh**

DECK	terraza **tehr-AH-sah**
DIG, TO	excava (you) **ex-KAH-vah** excavar (to) **ex-kah-VAR**
DIRT	la tierra **la tea-ER-rah**
DIRTY	sucio **sue-SEA-oh**
DISCONNECT	desconectar **des-co-neck-TAR**
DITCH	la zanja **la SAN-ha**
DOOR	la puerta **la PWEAR-tah**
DRAIN	el drenaje **el dren-AH-hay**
DRILL	taladro **tah-LA-dro**
DRIVEWAY	la entrada para carros **la en-TRA-dah** **PAH-rah CAR-rohs**

CONSTRUCTION

DROP, TO	dejar **day-HAR** caer **caw-ERR**
DRY	seco **SEH-co**
EDGE	filo **FEE-lo** borde **BORE-deh**
ELECTRICITY	la electricidad **la el-ehc-tree-see-DAHD**
EXPERIENCE, DO YOU HAVE?	¿Tienes experiencia? **tea-EN-es ex-pehr-ee-ehn-SEE-ah**
EXTEND	extender **ex-tend-EHR**
EXTERIOR	el exterior **el ex-teh-ree-ORE**
FAN	el abanico **el ah-bahn-EE-co**
FAUCET	la llave **la YAH-veh**

FEET	los pies **los PEE-es**
FINISH, TO	acabar **ah-cah-BAHR** terminar **tehr-mee-NAHR**
FIRE	el fuego **el FWAY-go**
FIX, TO	arreglar **ah-reg-LAHR** componer **comb-po-NEHR**
FLOOR	el piso **el PEE-soh**
FOOT	el pie **el PEE-eh**
FOOTINGS	cimientos **see-me-EN-tohs**
FORM	forma **FOR-mah**
FOUNDATION	la fundación **la foon-dah-see-ON**
FRAME, TO	formar **for-MAR**

CONSTRUCTION

FRAMING	formando **for-MAHN-do**
GATE	la puerta **la PWEAR-tah**
GLASS (PANE)	vidrio **vee-DREE-oh**
GLUE, TO	pega (you) **PAY-gah** pegar (to) **pay-GAR**
GLUE	resistol **ray-sees-TOHL**
GRADE, TO	emparejar **em-pah-ray-HAR**
GRAVEL	cascajo **cahs-CAH-hoe** grava **GRAH-vah**
GROOVE	muesca **MWES-cah**

SPANISH ON THE JOB

HACKSAW	sierra para cortar metal **see-ER-rah PAH-rah** **core-TAR may-TALL**
HAMMER	el martillo **el mahr-TEE-yo**
HANDLE (TOOL)	el mango **el MAHN-go**
HANG, TO	colgar **cohl-GAR**
HARD HAT	sombrero duro **sohm-BREH-roh DO-roh**
HAUL, TO	jala (you) **HAH-la** jalar (to) **hah-LAR**
HELP, TO	ayudar **ah-you-DAR**
HOLE	el hoyo **el OY-yo** el agujero **el ah-goo-HAIR-oh**
HOSE	la manguera **la mahn-GEH-rah**

CONSTRUCTION

INCH(ES)	pulgada(s) **pool-GAH-dah(s)**
INSULATION	insulación **in-sue-la-see-OHN**
JACK	el gato **el GAH-toh** hidráulico **ee-DRAUL-ee-co**
JACKHAMMER	martillo de presión de aire **mar-TEE-yoh deh** **pres-ee-OHN deh EYE-rey**
JAMB	jamba **HAHM-bah** marco para puerta **MAR-coh PAH-rah** **PWEAR-tah**
JOINT	unión **oo-knee-ON**
LACQUER	laca **LA-cah**
LADDER	la escalera **la es-cah-LEH-rah**
LEVEL, TO BE	a nivel **ah knee-VELL**

SPANISH ON THE JOB

LEVEL (TOOL)	el nivel **el knee-VELL** o la regla **oh la REG-lah**
LIFT, TO	subir **sue-BEER** levantar **leh-vahn-TAR** alzar **all-CZAR**
LIGHT	la luz **la loose**
LINE	la línea **la LEE-nay-ah**
LOCK, TO	cierra con llave (you) **see-ER-rah cone YAH-vay** cerrar (to) **sehr-RAHR**
LUMBER	la madera **la mah-DEH-rah**
MARK, TO	marcar **mar-CAR**
MEASURE, TO	medir **meh-DEER**

CONSTRUCTION

MESH (WIRE)	malla de acero **MAH-yah deh** **ah-CZEH-roh**
MEASUREMENT	la medida **la meh-DEE-dah**
MIX, TO	mezclar **mehz-CLAHR**
MORTAR	mezcla **MEHZ-clah**
NAIL	el clavo **el CLAH-voh**
NOTCH, CUT A	muesca **MWES-cah**
ORGANIZE, TO TIDY UP	organiza (you) **or-gah-KNEE-sah** organizar (to) **or-gah-knee-SAR**
PAINT	pintura **peen-TOO-rah**
PAINT, TO	pintar **peen-TAR**
PAINTBRUSH	cepillo de pintar **seh-PEE-yoh** **deh peen-TAR**

SPANISH ON THE JOB

PAINTER	pintor **peen-TORE**
PARALLEL	paralelo **pah-rah-LAY-low**
PATIO	el patio **el pah-TEA-oh**
PAVEMENT	el pavimento **el pah-vee-MEN-toe**
PICK (TOOL)	el pico **el PEE-koh**
PIPE	la pipa **la PEE-pah** el tubo **el TOO-bow**
PLANE (TOOL)	el cepillo **el seh-PEE-yoh** la garlopa **la gar-LOH-pah**
PLANS	los planos **lohs PLAH-nohs**
PLASTER	yeso **YEH-soh**

CONSTRUCTION

PLASTIC	plástico **PLAHS-tee-coh**
PLIERS	pinzas **PEEN-sahs**
PLUG, TO (A HOLE)	tapar **tah-PAR** resinar **reh-see-NAR**
PLUMB	plomada **plo-MAH-dah**
PLUMBER	plomero **plo-MAY-roh**
PLYWOOD	triply **TREE-ply**
POOL	la alberca **la ahl-BEHR-cah**
POST	el poste **el POH-steh**
PUTTY	masilla para resenar **mah-SEE-yah PAH-rah** **reh-seh-NAHR**
RAFTER	viga **VEE-gah**

SPANISH ON THE JOB

RAMP	la rampa **la RAHM-pah**
REMOVE, TO	quitar **key-TAR**
ROCK	la piedra **la pee-EH-drah**
ROOF	el techo **el TEH-cho**
ROOM	el cuarto **el KWAR-toh**
SAND	la arena **la ah-REH-nah**
SANDPAPER	el papel de lija **el pah-PEL deh LEE-ha**
SAW	el serrucho **el seh-ROO-cho**
SCAFFOLD	andamio **ahn-DAHM-ee-oh**
SCRAPER	raspador **rah-spah-DOOR**

CONSTRUCTION

SCREEN	mosquitero **mohs-key-TEH-roh** escren **es-CREHN**
SCREW	el tornillo **el tore-KNEE-yo**
SEWER	drenaje **dreh-NAH-hay**
SHOVEL	la pala **la PAH-la**
SINK	el fregadero **el freh-gah-DEH-roh**
SLAB	piso de cemento **PEE-soh deh** **seh-MEN-toh**
SPLICE, TO	empalmar **em-pahl-MAR**
SQUARE	cuadrado **kwah-DRAW-doh**
STAIRS	las escaleras **lahs es-cah-LEH-rahs**

SPANISH ON THE JOB

STAPLES	grapas **GRAH-pahs** grampas **GRAHM-pahs**
STAPLE, TO	engrapar **ehn-grah-PAR**
STEEL	acero **ah-SEH-roh**
STEP (STAIR)	escalón **es-cah-LONE**
STRAIGHT	derecho **deh-REH-cho**
STRETCH, TO	estirar **es-tea-RAHR**
STUCCO	estuco **es-TOO-co**
TAPE	la cinta **la SEEN-tah**
TAPE MEASURE	cinta de medir **SEEN-tah deh may-DEER**

CONSTRUCTION

TAR	brea **BRAY-ah** chapapote **chah-pah-POH-tay**
TILE	la teja **la TAY-ha**
TIME	tiempo **tee-EM-poh**
TOILET	el excusado **el es-coo-SAH-doe**
TOOLS	las herramientas **lahs err-ah-me-EN-tahs**
TOOL BOX	la caja de herramientas **la CAH-hah deh err-ah-me-EN-tahs**
TORCH	la antorcha **la ahn-TOR-cha**
TRASH	la basura **la bah-SOO-rah**
TRENCH	fosa **FOE-sa** zanja **SAN-ha**

SPANISH ON THE JOB

TRIM	moldura **mole-DO-rah**
TROWEL	llana **YAH-nah** flota de mano **FLO-tah deh MAH-no**
TRUCK	el camión **el cah-me-ON**
UNDERGROUND	subterráneo **soob-tehr-RAH-neh-oh**
UNEVEN	desigual **dehs-ee-GWAL**
UNLOAD, TO	descargar **dehs-car-GAHR**
WALL	la pared **la pah-RED**
WALLPAPER	papel de entapizar **pah-PEL deh en-tah-pee-CZAR**
WINDOW	la ventana **la ven-TAH-nah**
WIRE	el alambre **el ah-LAHM-bray**

CONSTRUCTION

WOOD	la madera **la mah-DEH-rah**
WORK	trabajo **trah-BAH-hoe**
WORKER	trabajador **trah-bah-ha-DOOR** obrero **oh-BRAY-roh**
WRENCH	llave inglesa **YAH-veh in-GLEH-sah**

SPANISH ON THE JOB

NOTES:

_____

_____

_____

_____

_____

_____

_____

_____

_____

_____

_____

_____

_____

_____

_____

_____

_____

_____

Part III

LANDSCAPING

LANDSCAPING

LANDSCAPING	JARDINERÍA har-dee-neh-RE-ah
ANTS	las hormigas **las ohr-ME-gahs**
APRICOT	el chabacano **el cha-bah-CAH-noh**
APPLE	la manzana **la man-SAH-nah**
APPLY, TO	aplica (you) **ah-PLEE-cah** aplicar (to) **ah-plee-CAR**
AVOCADO	el aguacate **el ah-gwah-CAH-teh**
AXE	el hacha **el AH-cha**
BAG	la bolsa **la BOWL-sah**
BARK CHIPS	los pedazos de corteza **lohs peh-DAH-sohs deh cor-TEH-sah**
BENCH	el banco **el BAHN-coh**

SPANISH ON THE JOB

BLADE (MOWER)	la hoja **la OH-ha** la navaja **la nah-VAH-ha**
BLOWER	el soplador **el soh-plah-DOOR**
BRICK	el ladrillo **el la-DREE-yoh**
BROKEN	quebrado **kay-BRAH-doh** roto **ROW-toe**
BROOM	la escoba **la es-CO-bah**
BUD	el brote **el BROH-teh** el botón **el boh-TOHN**
BULB	el bulbo **el BOOL-boh**
BUSH	el arbusto **el ahr-BOOS-toh**
CHAIN SAW	sierra de cadena **see-ER-rah deh cah-DEH-nah**

LANDSCAPING

CHEMICAL	la química **la KEY-me-cah**
CHERRY	la cereza **la say-REY-sah**
CHOP, TO	cortar **core-TAR** tajar **ta-HAR**
CLEAN UP, TO	limpiar **leem-pee-ARE**
CLIMB UP, TO	subir **sue-BEER**
COMPOST	el abono **el ah-BOH-no**
CONCRETE	el concreto **el cohn-CREH-toh**
CUT, TO	cortar **core-TAR**
CUTTINGS (to grow)	podos **POH-dohs**

DECK	cubierta **coo-bee-ERR-tah** terraza **tehr-RAH-sah**
DIG, TO	excava (you) **es-CAH-vah** excavar (to) **es-cah-VAR**
DIRT	la tierra **la tee-ER-rah**
DITCH	la zanja **la SAHN-ha**
DRAINAGE	drenaje **dreh-NAH-hay**
DRIP, TO	gotear **go-tay-ARE**
DRIVEWAY	entrada para carros **en-TRAH-dah** **PAH-rah CAR-rohs**
DRY., IT IS	Está seco. **es-TAH SEH-coh**
DUMP, TO	tira (you) **TEA-rah** tirar (to) **tea-RAHR**

LANDSCAPING

EDGE, TO	ribetear **re-beh-teh-ARE**
ENGINE	el motor **el mow-TORE** la máquina **la MAH-key-nah**
EROSION	erosión **el-roh-see-OHN** derrumbe **der-ROOM-bay**
FENCE	la cerca **la SERR-cah** el cerco **el SERR-coh**
FERTILIZER	abono **ah-BOW-no**
FLOWERS	las flores **lahs FLOH-rehs**
FLOWERBED	florido **floh-REH-doh**
FOLIAGE	follaje **foe-YAH-hay**

SPANISH ON THE JOB

FROST	helada **eh-LAH-dah** escarcha **es-CAR-chah**
FRUIT	la fruta **la FRU-tah**
GARAGE	el garaje **el gah-RAH-hay**
GARDEN	el jardín **el har-DEEN**
GARDENER	jardinero **har-deen-EH-roh**
GAS	gas **gahs**
GATE	la entrada **la** **ehn-TRAH-dah**
GLOVES	los guantes **lohs GWAN-tehs**
GRAPEFRUIT	la toronja **la toh-ROHN-ha**
GRASS	cespéd **sehs-PED** el sacate **el sah-CAH-teh**

LANDSCAPING

GRAVEL	cascajo **cahs-CAH-hoe** grava **GRAH-vah**
GREENHOUSE	invernadero **en-vehr-nah-DEH-roh**
GROW, TO (A CROP)	plantar **plahn-TAR**
GROW, TO	cultivar **cool-tee-VAR**
HANDLE (TOOL)	el mango **el MAHN-go**
HEDGE	el seto **el SET-oh**
HOE	el azadón **el ah-sah-DOHN**
HOLE	el hoyo **el OH-yo** el agujero **el ah-goo-HEH-roh**
HOSE	la manguera **la man-GEH-rah**
INSECT	el insecto **el in-SEC-toh**

SPANISH ON THE JOB

INSECTICIDE	la insecticida **la in-sec-tee-SEED-ah**
INSTALL, TO	instalar **in-stah-LAR**
IRRIGATION	irrigación **ir-ee-gah-cee-OHN**
IVY	la hiedra **la ee-EH-dra**
LABORER	trabajador **trah-bah-ha-DOOR**
LAND	terreno **tehr-REH-noh**
LANDSCAPE, TO	hacer el jardín **ah-SEHR el har-DEEN**
LAWN	césped **SEHS-ped** prado **PRAH-doe**
LAWN MOWER	cortadora de sacate **cor-tah-DOH-rah deh sa-CAH-teh**

LANDSCAPING

LEAVES	las hojas **lahs OH-hass**
LEMON	el limón **el lee-MOHN**
LETTUCE	la lechuga **la leh-CHOO-gah**
LIGHTS	las luces **lahs LOOS-es**
LIMB	la rama **la RAH-mah**
LIME	la lima **la LEE-mah** el límon **el LEE-mohn**
MAINTENANCE	mantenimiento **mahn-teh-nee-mee-EHN-toe**
MANURE	estiércol **es-tea-ERR-cohl**
MOW THE GRASS	cortar el sacate **core-TAR el sah-CAH-teh**

SPANISH ON THE JOB

NECTARINE	la nectarina **la neck-tah-REE-nah**
NOZZLE	tobera **toe-BEH-rah**
NURSERY	nurseria **nur-seh-REE-ah**
OIL	aceite **ah-seh-EE-teh**
ORANGE	naranja **nah-RAHN-ha**
OVERWATER, DON'T	no poner demasiado agua **no poh-NEHR** **deh-mah-see-AH-doe** **AH-gwah**
PALM(S)	la(s) palma(s) **la(hs) PAHL-ma(s)**
PARK	el parque **el PAR-kay**
PATH	la senda **la SEN-dah** vereda **veh-RAY-dah**

LANDSCAPING

PATIO	el patio **el pah-TEE-oh**
PAVEMENT	el pavimento **el pah-vee-MENT-oh** asfalto **ahs-FALL-toh**
PEACH	el durazno **el do-RAHS-no**
PICK, TO	escoger **es-coh-HERR** piscar **pees-KAR**
PINE	el pino **el PEA-no**
PIPE	la pipa **la PEA-pah**
PLANT(S)	la(s) planta(s) **lah(s) PLANH-tah(s)**
PLANT, TO	plantar **plahn-TAR**
POISON	el veneno **el veh-NEHN-oh**
POLE	el palo **el PAH-lo**

SPANISH ON THE JOB

POND	la charca **la CHAR-cah**
POOL	la alberca **la ahl-BEAR-cah**
POST	el poste **el POS-teh**
POT	la maceta **la ma-SAY-tah**
POTTING SOIL	la tierra abonada para jardín **la tea-ER-rah** **ah-bow-NAH-dah** **PAH-rah har-DEEN**
POWER	poder **poh-DARE** potencia **poh-ten-SEE-ah** electricidad **eh-lec-tree-see-DAHD**
PREPARE	prepara (you) **preh-PAH-rah** preparar (to) **preh-pah-RAHR**
PRUNE, TO	podar **poh-DAHR**

LANDSCAPING

PRUNE, CAN YOU?	¿Puede podar? **PWAY-deh poh-DAHR**
PUMP	bomba **BOHM-bah**
RAIN	la lluvia **la you-VEE-ah**
RAKE	rastrillo **rahs-TREE-yo**
RAKE, TO	rastrillar **rahs-tree-YAHR**
REMOVE, TO	remover **ray-mow-VEHR** quitar **key-TAR**
REPAIR, TO	reparar **ray-pah-RAHR**
REPLACE, TO	reponer **ray-poh-NEHR**
RETAINING WALL	la pared de retención **la pah-RED deh reh-ten-see-OHN**
RIPE	maduro **mah-DOO-roh**

SPANISH ON THE JOB

ROCKS	las piedras **lahs pee-EH-drahs**
ROOF	el techo **el TEH-cho**
ROOT(S)	la raíz **la rah-EES** las raíces **lahs rah-EE-sehs**
ROPE	la soga **la SOH-gah** la cuerda **la KWER-dah** el mecate **el meh-CAH-teh**
ROSE	la rosa **la ROH-sah**
ROTO-TILLER	aflojador de tierra **ah-flo-hah-DOOR deh tea-ER-rah**
SAND	la arena **la ah-REH-nah**
SAUCER	el platillo **el plah-TEE-yoh**
SAW (HAND)	serrucho de mano **sehr-ROO-cho deh MAH-no**

LANDSCAPING

SEED	la semilla **la seh-ME-yah**
SHADE	la sombra **la SOHM-bra**
SHAPE, TO	formar **for-MAHR**
SHOVEL	la pala **la PAH-la**
SHRUB	el arbusto **el ahr-BOO-stoh**
SIDEWALK	la banqueta **la bahn-KAY-tah**
SLOPE	declive **deh-CLEE-vay** ladera **la-DEH-rah**
SMOOTH	liso **LEE-so** suave **SWAH-vay**
SNAIL	el baboso **el bah-BO-soh**

SOAK, TO	empapar **em-pah-PAR** mojar demasiado **mow-HAR** **deh-mah-see-AH-doh**
SPRAY, TO	rociar **roh-see-ARE** fumigar **foo-me-GAHR**
SPRAYER	rociador **roh-see-ah-DOOR** bomba de fumigar **BOHM-bah deh foo-me-GAHR**
SPRINKLER	regadera **reh-gah-DEH-rah**
SPRINKLER SYSTEM	sistema de riego para jardín **see-STEH-mah deh** **ree-EH-go PAH-rah har-DEEN**
STACK, TO	apilar **ah-pee-LAHR** estacar **es-tah-CAR**
STAKE	la estaca **la es-TAH-cah**
STEM	el tallo **el TAH-yoh**

LANDSCAPING

STONE	la piedra **la pee-EH-drah**
STRAWBERRY	la fresa **la FREH-sah**
STUMP	el tronco **el TROHN-koh**
SUN	el sol **el sohl**
TANGERINE	la mandarina **la mahn-dah-REE-nah**
TILE (OUTDOOR)	loceta **low-SET-ah**
TOMATO	tomate **toh-MAH-teh**
TOOLS	las herramientas **lahs err-ah-me-EN-tahs**
TRACTOR	el tractor **el trahc-TOHR**

SPANISH ON THE JOB

TRANSPLANT, TO	transplantar **trahns-plahn-TAR**
TRASH, JUNK, GARBAGE	la basura **la bah-SOO-rah**
TRASHBAG	la bolsa para basura **la BOWL-sah PAH-rah bah-SOO-rah**
TRASHCAN	el bote de basura **el BOH-teh deh bah-SOO-rah**
TREE	el árbol **el AHR-bohl**
TREES	los árboles **los AHR-boh-lehs**
TRENCH	la zanja **la SAN-ha**
TRIM, TO	podar **poh-DAR**
TRIMMERS	podador **poh-dah-DOOR**
TRUNK	el tronco **el TROHN-koh**
UNDERGROUND	subterráneo **soob-tehr-RAH-neh-oh**

LANDSCAPING

UNLOAD, TO	descarga (you) **dehs-CAR-gah** descargar (to) **dehs-car-GAHR**
VALVE	la válvula **la VAHL-voo-lah**
VEGETABLE	vegetal **veh-heh-TAL**
VEGETABLES	las verduras **lahs vehr-DO-rahs**
WALL	la pared **la pah-RED**
WASH, TO	lavar **lah-VAR**
WATER, TO	regar **reh-GAHR**
WEED, TO	secar las hierbas **seh-CAR lahs ee-ER-bahs**
WEEDS	las malas hierbas **lahs MAH-lahs ee-ER-bahs**
WET	mojado **moh-HA-doh**
WHEELBARROW	la carretilla **la car-reh-TEE-yah**

SPANISH ON THE JOB

WIND	el viento **el vee-EN-toh** el aire **el EYE-rey**
WIRE	el alambre **el ah-LAHM-bray**
WOOD	la madera **la mah-DEH-rah**
YARD	la yarda **la YAR-dah** el patio **el pah-TE-yo**

Part IV

HOUSEKEEPING

HOUSEKEEPING

HOUSEKEEPING	SERVICIO DOMÉSTICO ser-VEE-see-oh do-MES-tee-co
APRON	el delantal **el deh-lahn-TALL** el mandil **el mahn-DEEL**
ASHES	la ceniza **la seh-NEE-sah**
ASHTRAY	el cenicero **el seh-nee-SEH-roh**
ASLEEP	dormido **dohr-ME-doh**
BABY BOTTLE	tetero **teh-TEH-roh**
BARBECUE	la barbacoa **la bar-bah-COH-ah**
BATHROOM	el baño **el BAHN-yoh**
BATHTUB	la bañera **la bahn-NYEH-rah**
BED	la cama **la CAH-mah**
BEDROOM	la recámara **la reh-CAH-mah-rah**

SPANISH ON THE JOB

BEDSPREAD	el sobrecama **el soh-breh-CAH-mah** la colcha **la COHL-cha**
BLANKET	la cobija **la co-BEE-ha**
BLEACH, TO	blanquear **blahn-kay-ARE**
BLEACH (PRODUCT)	el cloro **el CLOH-roh**
BOOK	el libro **el LEE-broh**
BOWL	la vasija **la vah-SEE-ha**
BOX	la caja **la CAH-ha**
BROOM	la escoba **la es-COH-bah**
BRUSH	el cepillo **el seh-PEE-yoh**
BUCKET	la cubeta **la coo-BEH-tah** el balde **el BAHL-deh**

HOUSEKEEPING

BURNER (ON STOVE)	el mechero **el meh-CHEH-roh** el quemador **el kay-mah-DOOR**
BUTTON	el botón **el boh-TOHN**
CAN	la lata **la LAH-tah**
CARPET	la carpeta **la car-PET-ah** la alfombra **la al-FOAM-brah**
CART	la carreta **la cahr-REH-tah**
CHAIR	la silla **la SEE-yah**
CLEAN, TO	limpia (you) **leem-PEE-ah** limpiar (to) **leem-pee-ARE**
CLEANER (PRODUCT)	limpiadora **leem-pee-ah-DOOR-ah**

SPANISH ON THE JOB

CLEAR THE TABLE	leventar la mesa **leh-vehn-TAR la MEH-sah**
CLOSET	el ropero **el roh-PEH-roh**
CLOTHES	la ropa **la ROH-pah**
CLOTHES LINE	la línea de ropa **la LEE-knee-ah deh ROH-pah**
COFFEE	el café **el kah-FEY**
COLD	frío **FREE-yo**
COUCH	la sofá **la soh-FAH** el sillón **el see-YON**
COUNTER	mostrador **mohs-trah-DOOR**
COVER, TO	cubrir **coo-BREER**
CRIB	la cuna **la COO-nah**

HOUSEKEEPING

CUP	la taza **la TAH-sah**
CUPBOARDS	los gabinetes **lohs gahb-ee-NET-ehs**
CURTAINS (DRAPES)	las cortinas **lahs cohr-TEE-nahs**
DESK	el escritorio **el es-cree-TOHR-ree-oh**
DINING ROOM	el comedor **el coh-meh-DOOR**
DIAPER	el pañal **el pahn-YAL**
DIRTY	sucio **soo-SEE-oh**
DISHES, PLATES	los platos **lohs PLAH-tohs** los trastes **lohs TRAHS-tehs**
DISHWASHER (MACHINE OR PERSON)	el lavaplatos **el lah-vah-PLAH-tohs**
DOOR	la puerta **la PWEHR-tah**

DOWNSTAIRS	abajo **ah-BAH-hoh**
DRAINBOARD	el escurreplatos **el es-coor-reh-PLAH-tohs**
DRAWER	el cajón **el cah-HOHN**
DRESSER	el tocador **el tohk-ah-DOOR**
DRY, TO	secar **seh-CAR**
DRYER (MACHINE)	el secador **el seh-cah-DOOR**
DUST	el polvo **el POHL-voh**
DUST, TO	sacudir **sah-coo-DEER**
DUSTPAN	el cogedor **el co-hay-DOOR**
EMPTY, TO	vaciar **vah-see-ARE**
FAMILY ROOM	el cuarto de família **el KWAR-toh deh** **fah-MEE-lee-ah**

HOUSEKEEPING

FAN	el abanico **el ah-bahn-EE-coh**
FAUCET	la llave **la YAH-veh**
FINGERPRINTS	las huellas **lahs WHAY-yahs**
FIRE	el fuego **el FWAY-goh**
FIREPLACE	la chimenea **la chee-meh-NAY-ah**
FIREWOOD	la leña **la LAY-nyah**
FLAME	la lumbre **la LOOM-bray**
FLOOR	el piso **el PEE-soh**
FOLD, TO	doblar **doh-BLAHR**
FOOD	alimento **ah-lee-MEHN-toh**
FORK	el tenedor **el ten-eh-DOOR**

SPANISH ON THE JOB

FREEZER	el helador **el eh-lah-DOOR** el congelador **el cohn-hel-ah-DOOR**
FURNITURE	los muebles **lohs MWAY-blehs**
GARAGE	el garaje **el gah-RAH-heh**
GLASS	el vidrio **el vee-DREE-oh**
GLASS (DRINKING)	el vaso **el VAH-so**
GLOVES	los guantes **lohs GWAHN-tehs**
GROCERIES	el mandado **el mahn-DAH-doh**
GUESTS	los huéspedes **los oo-AYS-peh-des**
GUEST ROOM	el cuarto de huésped **el KWAR-toh deh oo-AYS-ped**
HALLWAY	el pasillo **el pah-SEE-yo**

HOUSEKEEPING

HAMPER (CLOTHES BASKET)	el cesto de ropa **el SEHS-toh deh ROH-pah**
HANG, TO	colgar **cohl-GAHR**
HANGER	el gancho **el GAHN-cho**
HOT	caliente **kah-lee-EN-tay**
HOUSE	la casa **la CAH-sah**
ICE	el hielo **el ee-EL-oh**
ICE BUCKET	el cubo de hielo **el COO-boh deh ee-EL-oh**
IRON	la plancha **la PLAHN-cha**
IRON, TO	planchar **plahn-CHAR**
IRONING BOARD	tabla de planchar **TAH-bla deh plahn-CHAR** el burro **el BOOR-roh**

SPANISH ON THE JOB

JANITOR	el portero **el por-TEH-roh**
KEY	la llave **la YAH-vey**
KITCHEN	la cocina **la ko-SEE-nah**
KNIFE	el cuchillo **la coo-CHEE-yoh**
LADDER	la escalera **la es-cah-LEH-rah**
LAMP	la lámpara **la LAHM-pah-rah**
LAMPSHADE	la pantalla **la pahn-TAH-yah**
LAUNDRY	la lavandería **la lah-vahn-dehr-EE-ah**
LAUNDRY DETERGENT	el detergente **el deh-tehr-HEN-teh**
LAUNDRY ROOM	el cuarto de lavandería **el KWAR-toh deh lah-vahn-dehr-EE-ah**
LID	la tapadera **la tah-pah-DEH-rah**

HOUSEKEEPING

LIGHT	la luz **la loose**
LIGHT BULB	la bombilla **la bohm-BEE-yah**
LINEN	la ropa blanca **la ROH-pah BLAHN-ca**
LINEN CLOSET	el armario para ropa blancha **el are-mar-EE-oh PAH-rah ROH-pah BLAHN-cah**
LIVING ROOM	la sala **la SAH-lah**
LOBBY	el vestíbulo **el ves-TEE-boo-low**
LOCK	la cerradura **la sehr-rah-DO-rah**
LOCK, TO	cerrar con llave **sehr-RAHR cone YAH-veh**
MAGAZINE	la revista **la reh-VEES-tah**
MAID	la criada **la cree-AH-dah**

SPANISH ON THE JOB

MAKE THE BED, TO	tender la cama **tehn-DEHR la CAH-mah**
MARKET	el mercado **el mehr-CAH-doh**
MATCHES	los cerillos **lohs sehr-EE-yohs**
MATTRESS	el colchón **el cohl-CHOHN**
MEND, TO	remienda (you) **ray-me-EN-dah** remendar (to) **ray-men-DAHR**
MICROWAVE	la microhonda **la mee-croh-OHN-dah**
MILK	leche **LEH-chay**
MIRROR	es espejo **el es-PAY-ho**
MOP	el estropajo **el es-troh-PAH-hoh**
MOP, TO	mapear **mah-peh-AHR** trapear **trah-peh-AHR**

NAPKINS	las servilletas **lahs sehr-vee-YEH-tahs**
NEAT	ordenado **ohr-deh-NAH-doh**
NEEDLE	la aguja **la ah-GOO-ha**
NEWSPAPER	el periódico **el pehr-ee-OH-dee-coh**
OFFICE	la oficina **la oh-fee-SEE-nah**
OVEN	el horno **el OHR-no**
PANS	las cacerolas **lahs cah-seh-ROH-lahs** los sartenes **lohs sahr-TEH-nehs**
PANTS	los pantalones **lohs pahn-tah-LONE-es**
PAPER	el papel **el pah-PEHL**
PAPER TOWEL	la toalla de papel **la toh-AH-yah** **deh pah-PELL**

SPANISH ON THE JOB

PEPPER	la pimienta **la pee-me-EN-tah**
PICTURE	el cuadro **el KWAH-droh**
PILLOW	la almohada **la ahl-moh-AH-dah**
PILLOWCASE	la funda **la FOON-dah**
POISON	el veneno **el veh-NEH-noh**
POLISH, TO	pulir (to) **poo-LEER** lustre (you) **LOOS-treh** lustrar (to) **loos-TRAHR**
POTS	las ollas **las OH-yas**
RADIO	el radio **el RAH-de-oh**
RAG	el trapo **el TRAH-po**
REFRIGERATOR	el refrigerador **el reh-free-hey-rah-DOOR**

HOUSEKEEPING

RESTROOM	el baño **el BAHN-yoh**
RINSE, TO	enjuaga (you) **en-HWAH-gah** enjuagar (to) **en-hwah-GAR**
ROOM	el cuarto **el KWAR-toh**
RUG	la alfombra **la al-FOAM-brah**
SALT	la sal **la sahl**
SAND	la arena **la ah-REH-nah**
SCRAPE, TO	raspar **rahs-PAR** rascar **rahs-CAR**
SCISSORS	las tijeras **lahs tee-HEH-rahs**
SCRUB, TO	restregar **rehs-treh-GAHR** fregar **freh-GAHR**

SPANISH ON THE JOB

SET THE TABLE	poner la mesa **poh-NEHR la MEH-sah**
SEW, TO	coser **coh-SEHR**
SHAKE, TO	sacudir **sah-coo-DEER**
SHAMPOO	el champú **el cham-POO**
SHEETS	las sábanas **lahs SAH-bah-nahs**
SHELF	el estante **el es-TAHN-teh** la repisa **la reh-PEE-sah**
SHIRT	la camisa **la cah-MEE-sah**
SHOES	los zapatos **lohs sah-PAH-tohs**
SHOPPING	ir de compras **ear deh COHM-prahs**
SHOWER	la ducha **la DOO-cha**

SIDEWALK	la acera **la ah-SEH-rah**
SILVERWARE	los cubiertos **lohs coo-bee-EHR-tohs**
SINK	el fregadero **el freh-gah-DEH-roh**
SMOKE, TO	fumar **foo-MAHR**
SOAK	empapar **em-pah-PAHR**
SOAP	el jabón **el hah-BOHN**
SOCKS	el calcetín **el cahl-seh-TEEN**
SPOON	la cuchara **la coo-CHAH-rah**
SPONGE	la esponja **la ehs-POHN-ha**
SPOT, STAIN	la mancha **la MAHN-cha**
STAIRS	las escaleras **lahs es-cah-LEH-rahs**

SPANISH ON THE JOB

STOVE	la estufa **la es-TOO-fah**
SUGAR	el azúcar **el ah-SOO-car**
SUIT	el traje **el TRAH-hay**
SUITCASE	la maleta **lah mah-LEH-tah**
SWEEP, TO	barre (you) **BAH-rey** barrer (to) **bah-REHR**
TABLE	la mesa **la MEH-sah**
TELEPHONE	el teléfono **el teh-LEH-phon-oh**
TELEVISION	la televisión **la teh-leh-vee-see-OHN**
THREAD	el hilo **el EE-loh**
TILE	la teja **la TEH-ha**

HOUSEKEEPING

TOASTER	el tostador **el tohs-tah-DOOR**
TOILET	el excusado **el es-coo-SAH-doh**
TOILET PAPER	papel higiénico **pah-PEL ee-he-EH-nee-co**
TOOLS	las herramientas **lahs err-ah-me-EN-tahs**
TOWELS	las toallas **lahs toh-AH-yahs**
TOYS	los juguetes **lohs who-GEH-tes**
TRASH	la basura **la bah-SOO-rah**
TRASHBAG	la bolsa para basura **la BOHL-sah PAH-rah bah-SOO-rah**
TRASHCAN	el bote de basura **el BOH-teh deh bah-SOO-rah**
TRAY	la bandeja **la bahn-DAY-hah**
UNDERWEAR	la ropa interior **la ROH-pah en-teh-ree-OHR**

SPANISH ON THE JOB

UNIFORM	el uniforme **el oo-nee-FOR-meh**
UPSTAIRS	arriba **ah-REE-bah**
VACUUM	la aspiradora **la ah-spee-rah-DOOR-ah**
VACUUM BAG	la bolsa **la BOHL-sah**
WALL	la pared **la pah-RED**
WARM	tibio **TEE-bee-oh**
WASH, TO	lavar **lah-VAHR**
WASHING MACHINE	la lavadora **la lah-vah-DOOR-ah**
WATER	el agua **el AH-gwah**
WAX	la cera **la SEH-rah**

HOUSEKEEPING

WAX, TO	encerar **en-seh-RAHR**
WOOD	la madera **la mah-DEH-rah**
WORK	el trabajo **el trah-BAH-ho**